BASIC / NOT BORING
LANGUAGE SKILLS

GRAMMAR & USAGE

Grades 6–8⁺

Inventive Exercises to Sharpen
Skills and Raise Achievement

Series Concept & Development
by Imogene Forte & Marjorie Frank
Exercises by Joy MacKenzie

Incentive Publications, Inc.
Nashville, Tennessee

About the cover:
   Bound resist, or tie dye, is the most ancient known method
   of fabric surface design. The brilliance of the basic tie dye
   design on this cover reflects the possibilities that emerge
   from the mastery of basic skills.

Illustrated by Kathleen Bullock
Cover art by Mary Patricia Deprez, dba Tye Dye Mary®
Cover design by Marta Drayton, Joe Shibley, and W. Paul Nance
Edited by Anna Quinn

ISBN 978-0-86530-362-1

8   9   10   12   11   10   09

PRINTED IN THE UNITED STATES OF AMERICA
www.incentivepublications.com

TABLE OF CONTENTS

CELEBRATE BASIC GRAMMAR & USAGE SKILLS

Basic does not mean boring! There certainly is nothing dull about joining a bunch of wacky characters at the beach and using grammar skills to find . . .

> . . . coded messages sent by ships in distress
>
> . . . clauses caught in lobster claws
>
> . . . ocean-bottom nouns lost in a coral maze
>
> . . . divers spearing transitive and intransitive verbs
>
> . . . shark-sighting adverbs
>
> . . . commas lost (along with swim suits) in the wild surf
>
> . . . subjects and verbs that are more (or less) disagreeable than crabs

The idea of celebrating the basics—enjoying and improving the basic skills of grammar and usage—is an important concept to convey to students. The pages that follow are full of exercises for students that will help to review and strengthen specific, basic skills in the content area of language. This is not just another ordinary "fill-in-the-blanks" way to learn. The high-interest activities will put students to work applying a rich variety of the most important knowledge and skills for grammar and English usage while enjoying fun and challenging adventures with words, punctuation marks, and beach-related adventures.

The pages in this book can be used in many ways:
- for individual students to sharpen a particular skill
- with a small group needing to relearn or strengthen a skill
- as an instructional tool for teaching a skill to any size group
- by students working on their own
- by students working under the direction of an adult

Each page may be used to introduce a new skill, reinforce a skill, or assess a student's ability to perform a skill. And, there's more than just the forty pages of great student activities! You'll also find a hearty appendix of resources helpful for students and teachers—including a ready-to-use test for assessing these grammar and usage skills.

As students take on the challenges of these adventures with grammar and usage, they will sharpen their mastery of basic skills and will enjoy learning to the fullest. And as you watch them check off the basic grammar and usage skills they've strengthened, you can celebrate with them!

SKILLS CHECKLIST FOR GRAMMAR & USAGE

✔	SKILL	PAGE(S)
	Identify declarative, interrogative, imperative, exclamatory sentences	10
	Find subjects and predicates	11
	Identify simple, complex, and compound sentences	14
	Correct sentence fragments and run-on sentences	12
	Identify parts of speech	13, 14, 28, 29
	Identify and use common and proper nouns	15
	Identify and use singular and plural nouns	16
	Identify, form, and use possessive nouns	17
	Identify and use different kinds of pronouns	18, 19, 20
	Identify and use proper pronoun-antecedent agreement	19
	Properly use *who, whom, who's,* and *whose*	20
	Identify and use verb tenses	21
	Identify and use action verbs and verbs of being (linking verbs)	21, 22
	Identify and use regular and irregular verbs	23
	Identify and use transitive and intransitive verbs	24
	Identify and use direct and indirect objects	25
	Properly use special verbs such as *lie and lay, sit and set, rise and raise*	26
	Understand and use subject-verb agreement	27
	Identify and use adjectives	28
	Identify and use adverbs	29
	Identify and use comparative and superlative adjectives and adverbs	30
	Identify and correct dangling modifiers	31
	Use negatives correctly; correct double negatives	32
	Identify and use prepositions and prepositional phrases	33
	Identify and use participles and participial phrases	34
	Identify and use gerund and infinitive phrases	35, 36
	Identify and use independent and dependent clauses	37
	Identify and use noun, adjective, and adverb clauses	38
	Use proper capitalization for proper nouns and adjectives	39
	Properly use a variety of punctuation marks	40-48
	Use proper punctuation and capitalization for a variety of situations	39-48
	Make corrections in improper punctuation	39-48
	Use commas properly in a variety of situations	44
	Use quotation marks properly in dialogue	45
	Use colons and semicolons properly	46
	Use hyphens, dashes, and parentheses properly	47
	Create, explain, and properly punctuate common contractions	48

GRAMMAR & USAGE

Skills Exercises

GRAMMAR IN
A BOTTLE

SURF'S UP!

When surfers yell, "Surf's up!" they're using a particular kind of sentence. Do you know which kind?

> There are four kinds of sentences: **declarative (D), interrogative (?),**
> **imperative (I)** and **exclamatory (E).**

Use the appropriate mark to identify each sentence below.
Then add the correct punctuation at the end of each line.

_____ 1. Surf's up

_____ 2. We're off to the beach

_____ 3. Skiers should watch for shark activity

_____ 4. Has anyone seen the lifeguard

_____ 5. Watch out for the jellyfish

_____ 6. If you want to jet ski, get to the dock by noon

_____ 7. Did you know there was recently a Loch Ness
Monster sighted in this area

_____ 8. The trouble with beaches is that they are so sandy

_____ 9. Watch for fiddler crabs

_____ 10. They pinch

_____ 11. I love to walk on the beach at sundown

_____ 12. Anybody up for beach volleyball

_____ 13. What a thrill to get an Olympic gold medal

_____ 14. The sign says, "No dogs on the beach," so we better take Phil home

_____ 15. Thought for a night on the boardwalk: a fool and his money are soon parted

_____ 16. Who's ready for an Awesome Hot Dog

_____ 17. He or she who suns unprotected is seriously lacking in intellectual capacity

_____ 18. We creamed those girls in our surf contest

_____ 19. You can really chill out on a hot beach

_____ 20. How can you be cold and hot at the same time, silly

Name

10

ONE OF EACH

Every two-piece bathing suit has a top and a bottom—one of each! Every sentence has two parts, too—a subject and a predicate.

> The **subject** is the part of the sentence which is doing something or about which something is being said.
>
> The **predicate** is the part of the sentence that tells something about the subject.

I. In each sentence below, draw a single line under the complete subject; draw a double line under the complete predicate.

1. Hundreds of gulls were flying around the dock.
2. On rainy days, does the fog obliterate your view?
3. A whale's big, bulky body can be a fearsome sight.
4. A huge animal does not necessarily have a huge brain.
5. The giant whale leaped into the air and startled everyone.
6. Gory scenes on television have frightened some people away from ocean swimming.
7. Yesterday, three high school kids and two pelicans had a fishing contest.
8. Can you guess the results of the contest?
9. In spite of fair warning, the boys took the jet skis beyond the breakwater.
10. Why do teenage boys often ignore good advice?

II. In the numbered spaces below, write only the simple subject and simple verb for each sentence. Don't get fooled by one or two compound subjects or verbs!

1. _____ _____
2. _____ _____
3. _____ _____
4. _____ _____
5. _____ _____

6. _____ _____
7. _____ _____
8. _____ _____
9. _____ _____
10. _____ _____

Name _____

S.O.S. (SAVE OUR SENTENCES!)

At sea, distress is often expressed by signal flags. Fragments and run-on sentences are clearly in distress. For each sentence fragment or run-on, write the distress code S.O.S. For each sentence that is correct, write A.O.K. Save the distressed items by making the necessary corrections.

1. I dated a girl, she dumped me.

_____

2. I like hamburgers with mustard, catsup, pickle, and rock music.

_____

3. When I get pumped and ready for a great game.

_____

4. Beach music on the boardwalk by the sea.

_____

5. Are you heading for the Ferris wheel count me in?

_____

6. Dancing in the moonlight with a handsome hunk of the male species.

_____

7. All day, I lie in the sun and dream in golden bronze.

_____

8. Where did those bikers come from, San Francisco?

_____

9. Putting sand crabs in people's shoes.

_____

10. There's nothing I love more than wild surf, it is incredibly invigorating!

_____

The flags on the left show the International Alphabet in Flag Code. Use the flags to write a short message below. Draw a flag for each letter of each word.

_____

_____

_____

_____

Name _____

WHAT'S FOR LUNCH?

On a cold, foggy day at the seashore, there is nothing more comforting than a bowl of hot soup. Discover what soup is the special on today's menu by solving the puzzle and transferring the numbered letters to the corresponding spaces at the bottom of the page.

First, you must place each word in this list in its appropriate space:

yesterday	loiter	there	tough	nobody
fishing	skinny	regurgitate	illustrate	everything
wise	lighthouse	disappear	Maine	slowly

1. NOUN   __ __ __ __ __ __ __ __ __
           4

2. VERB   __ __ __ __ __ __
  2

3. ADJECTIVE   __ __ __ __ __ __
  8

4. ADVERB   __ __ __ __ __ __

5. PRONOUN   __ __ __ __ __ __ __ __ __ __

6. ADJECTIVE   __ __ __ __
  11

7. ADVERB   __ __ __ __ __

8. VERB   __ __ __ __ __ __ __ __ __ __ __
        6

9. NOUN   __ __ __ __ __ __ __

10. PRONOUN   __ __ __ __ __ __
  3

11. VERB   __ __ __ __ __ __ __ __ __
      7

12. ADJECTIVE   __ __ __ __ __
  9

13. ADVERB   __ __ __ __ __ __ __ __
   5

14. NOUN   __ __ __ __ __
   10

15. VERB   __ __ __ __ __ __ __ __
  1

Soup of the day: __ __ __ __ __ __ __   __ __ __ __
    1 2 3 4 5 6 7   8 9 10 11

Name

A-MAZE-ING POSSIBILITIES

The bottom of the sea is like a maze. Many interesting things are hidden among the rocks, plants, and coral.

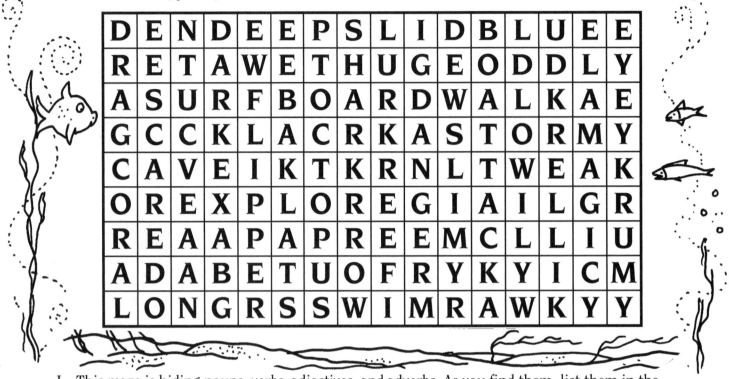

D	E	N	D	E	E	P	S	L	I	D	B	L	U	E	E
R	E	T	A	W	E	T	H	U	G	E	O	D	D	L	Y
A	S	U	R	F	B	O	A	R	D	W	A	L	K	A	E
G	C	C	K	L	A	C	R	K	A	S	T	O	R	M	Y
C	A	V	E	I	K	T	K	R	N	L	T	W	E	A	K
O	R	E	X	P	L	O	R	E	G	I	A	I	L	G	R
R	E	A	A	P	A	P	R	E	E	M	C	L	L	I	U
A	D	A	B	E	T	U	O	F	R	Y	K	Y	I	C	M
L	O	N	G	R	S	S	W	I	M	R	A	W	K	Y	Y

I. This maze is hiding nouns, verbs, adjectives, and adverbs. As you find them, list them in the proper category below. (Several words may fit in more than one category!)

NOUNS *(about 30)*	VERBS *(about 16)*	ADJECTIVES *(about 23)*	ADVERB *(only 1!)*

II. On the back side of this paper, use combinations of words from the lists above to create **two simple sentences**, **three complex sentences**, and **three compound sentences**. Check your grammar text to review the properties of each kind of sentence.

Name _____

TWO BY THE SEA

Crusty Old Pirate Patch-Eye has hidden his "treasures" in his chest. For each category, write two common nouns that tell what could be in there. All items must have some association with the beach or sea. The name of each item must begin with the letter at the top of each column.

Category	C	S
something to eat	1. _____	_____
item of clothing	2. _____	_____
animal	3. _____	_____

KEEP AWAY FROM ME TREASURE

Write any two sea-related common nouns for each of these:

Category	T	M
method of travel	4. _____	_____
game or sport	5. _____	_____
something belonging to a teenager	6. _____	_____

Write any two sea-related proper nouns for each of these:

Category	R	A
titles of songs, books, poems, or movies	7. _____	_____
name of a famous person (real or fictional)	8. _____	_____
something belonging to a teenager	9. _____	_____

Name _____

SEE YOU AT THE CLUB

The signs at the beach clubhouse are covered with plural nouns. Find them all! Then write each plural on a line below, followed by the matching rule (1, 2, 3, or 4) that governs that plural.

Rules for Forming Plural Nouns

1. Form most plurals by adding *s* to the singular noun.
2. If the singular noun ends in *s, ss, sh, ch,* or *x,* add *es* to form a plural noun.
3. If the noun ends in *y* preceded by a consonant, change the *y* to *i* and add *es.*
4. Some nouns, such as *man* or *mouse,* are formed irregularly.

	Plural	*Rule*		*Plural*	*Rule*
1.	_____	___	12.	_____	___
2.	_____	___	13.	_____	___
3.	_____	___	14.	_____	___
4.	_____	___	15.	_____	___
5.	_____	___	16.	_____	___
6.	_____	___	17.	_____	___
7.	_____	___	18.	_____	___
8.	_____	___	19.	_____	___
9.	_____	___	20.	_____	___
10.	_____	___	21.	_____	___
11.	_____	___	22.	_____	___

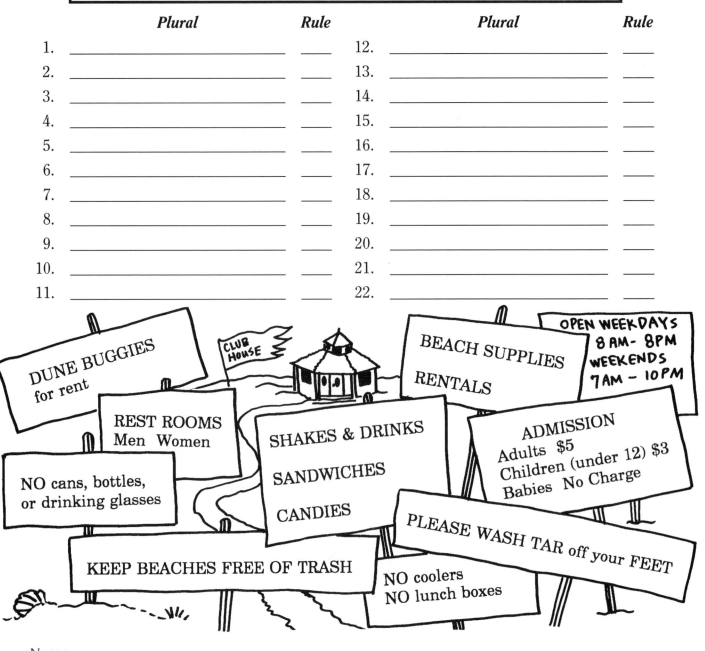

Name _____

SEASHORE SNAPSHOTS

The sights and sounds of the seashore make you want to grab your camera.

> To show that something belongs to a singlular person, place, or thing, add 's to the noun. To show ownership by more than one person, place, or thing add 's unless the plural ends in s. Then add only an apostrophe.

Close your eyes and pay attention to the mental snapshots created by each of these phrases. Then rephrase each one to make it show ownership.

1. Fin belonging to a shark _____

2. Whistles belonging to the lifeguards _____

3. Radio belonging to Gus _____

4. Surfboard belonging to somebody _____

5. Laughter of the children _____

6. Sounds made by the surf _____

7. Cries of the gulls _____

8. Suntans belonging to teenagers _____

9. Warnings sounded by bell buoys _____

10. Strength of ocean swimmers _____

11. Soles of sandals _____

12. The colorful sails of boats _____

13. The stories of footprints _____

14. Beach belonging to no one _____

Use the lines below to write a very short sea story in which you use at least ten possessive nouns, none of which are mentioned above. Underline each possessive in your story.

A VERY SHORT SEA STORY

_____
_____
_____
_____

Name _____

PICK A PRONOUN

You can't escape pronouns. They're everywhere. In the dunes, on the sand, under the water. They're usually little words, but there's a lot to remember about these little things. Show what you know about pronouns.

I. Match each item in Column A with its appropriate companion in Column B.

A	B
1. _____ pronoun	A. NOT referring to a particular person or thing
2. _____ relative pronoun	B. word for which the pronoun stands
3. _____ demonstrative pronoun	C. the self-selves forms of personal pronouns
4. _____ antecedent	D. used in questions
5. _____ compound pronoun	E. used to introduce adjective clauses
6. _____ indefinite pronoun	F. takes a plural verb
7. _____ interrogative pronoun	G. used to point out a specific person or thing
8. _____ each	H. used in place of one or more nouns
9. _____ personal pronoun	I. takes a singular verb
10. _____ reflexive pronoun	J. I, we, you, your, she, it, their

II. In each sentence, circle the antecedent for the pronoun(s) written in bold type.

1. Margaret lost her bathing suit; do you suppose an octopus ate **it**?
2. Jim watched the frisbee as **it** disappeared behind the dunes.
3. The ball touched the player's hands before he noticed the wasp perched on **it**.
4. Megan, stop chasing the boys; **you** boys stop chasing **her**.
5. The girl **who** had been hit by the dune buggy regained consciousness.

III. Copy each pronoun in bold type in the corresponding space below and tell what kind of pronoun it is.

1. **Who** is yelling from the cliffs?
2. It was Jeff's irresponsible action **that** caused the accident.
3. Now he hates **himself.**
4. **Those** are wonderful hot dogs.
5. **Whoever** put this crab in my bag is dead meat!

1. _____ _____
2. _____ _____
3. _____ _____
4. _____ _____
5. _____ _____

Name _____

THE AGREEABLE PRONOUN

Crabs aren't always agreeable. (People often see them fighting.)

> A pronoun must agree with its antecedent (the word it refers to) in number and gender.

I. Write the antecedent for each pronoun printed in bold.

1. Some of the students brought **their** lunches to the beach. _____

2. Ken took Meg home on **his** new motorcycle. _____

3. John and Eric blamed **themselves** for the accident. _____

4. The members of the class turned in **their** term papers. _____

5. We found a chambered nautilus and kept **it.** _____

6. Would you lend me **one** of your sweaters? _____

7. We keep the priceless vase in **its** special cabinet. _____

8. The divers found pieces of coral and brought **them** back to the boat. _____

9. We surprised **ourselves** by winning the sailing race. _____

10. We could have kept the trophy, but we shared **it.** _____

> Two or more singular antecedents joined by *or* or *nor* should be referred to by a singular pronoun. Two or more antecedents joined by *and* should be referred to by a plural pronoun.

II. Underline the correct pronoun and circle the antecedent(s).

1. None of the trees were destroyed in the storm, but (they, it) lost many branches.

2. The cats have (their, its) own personalities.

3. Someone put (their, her) sunglasses in the wrong bag.

4. The winds of the storm may blow (themselves, itself) out.

5. Both of Sue's sisters lost (her, their) purses.

6. Did either Libby or Danielle call about (their, her) appointment?

7. Neither Erin nor Scott ate (their, his) lunch.

8. Jim and Troy have made up (his, their) own minds.

9. Since when has a J-24 won (its, their) first race?

10. Every ship in the race chooses (its, their) own course.

WELL, HE'S AN AGREEABLE GUY

Name _____

WHO'S WHO?

Who's on the line? **Who's** calling for **whom? Who** wants to talk to **whose** friend?

> **Who** is used as the subject of a verb; **whom** is used as a direct object or the object of a preposition.
>
> **Who's** is the contraction for *who is*; **whose** is a possessive pronoun.

Circle the correct choice for each item.

1. (Who, Whom) ordered this pizza?

2. (Who's, Whose) wet towel is this?

3. For (who, whom) did you sacrifice your dill pickle?

4. (Who's, Whose) that joker with the sunburn?

5. The girl with (who, whom) I danced is very light on her feet.

6. (Who, Whom) may I say is calling?

7. (Who, Whom) do you think left this mess on the table?

8. The cousin about (who, whom) I spoke is going to college in the fall.

9. Did you ever hear of Hemingway, (who, whom) wrote *The Old Man and the Sea?*

10. (Who's, Whose) the author of *Jaws?*

11. (Whose, Who's) book is *Treasure Island?*

12. Do you know (who, whom) wrote *The Rime of the Ancient Mariner?*

13. The writer to (who, whom) you are referring is Coleridge.

14. I admire sailors of old (who, whom) I never met.

15. I remember best the teacher (who, whom) is responsible for my love of poetry.

16. I'm scared of anyone (whose, who's) not scared of *Jaws.*

17. The fish of (whom, who) you speak isn't even real!

18. Look (who's, whose) talking! You got out of the water when a minnow nibbled your feet.

19. Hey! (Who, Whom) do you think you are?

20. I'm someone (whom, who) everyone believes!

Name

TENSE TIMES

These pictures show some tense situations at sea. Tell each story by conjugating the verb in all its active tenses. The verb can be found near each picture.

DIVE
present _____
past _____
future _____
present perfect _____
past perfect _____
future perfect _____

WHOOPEE

I CAN'T STAND IT

STAND
present _____
past _____
future _____
present perfect _____
past perfect _____
future perfect _____

BLOWN
present _____
past _____
future _____
present perfect _____
past perfect _____
future perfect _____

FIGHT
present _____
past _____
future _____
present perfect _____
past perfect _____
future perfect _____

TAKE THAT!

HIDE
present _____
past _____
future _____
present perfect _____
past perfect _____
future perfect _____

SHUSH!

Name _____

Basic Skills/Grammar & Usage 6-8+   Copyright ©1997 by Incentive Publications, Inc., Nashville, TN.

WILD ABOUT VERBS

Victor is obsessed with verbs. No one knows how he got started, but he just can't stop going wild over verbs. You don't have to be a verb nerd to figure out which verbs are linking verbs and which are active verbs. Just remember this:

> A **linking verb** is a verb that does not show action, but serves as a link between two words. Linking verbs are sometimes called **verbs of being.**

Underline the verb in each sentence below.
If the verb is an **action verb**, write **A** on the line provided. If it is a **linking verb**, write **L**.

_____ 1. Victor is a verb nerd.

_____ 2. A verb nerd responds ecstatically to his favorite words—verbs.

_____ 3. Victor grows restless if he is deprived of a grammar book or dictionary.

_____ 4. He appears jittery when away from the sounds of verbs.

_____ 5. Victor often becomes hoarse from reciting lists of linking verbs.

_____ 6. He seems enervated from constantly demonstrating action verbs.

_____ 7. He rejoices gleefully when he hears a crowd yell, "Go!" to a team.

_____ 8. He's wild when a pitcher pitches and a catcher catches.

_____ 9. He watches flowers grow.

_____ 10. He listens to roosters crow.

_____ 11. Victor has plans for starting a verb choir.

_____ 12. The choir will sing only verbs.

_____ 13. He teaches verbs to his pet cockatiel.

_____ 14. He can sleep only with his verbaphone playing soft predicate phrases.

_____ 15. He often looks tired in the morning.

Name _____

FIN FAN FUN

Fisherman Franz **will throw** this little fish back in the water. He **threw** the last three back. In fact, he **has thrown** all the fish back that he's caught today.

Throw is an irregular verb. The past and past participle forms do not follow the usual rules. For each of the irregular verbs below, write the missing form(s). You may need your grammar text to help with the answers.

verb	past	past participle
1. catch	_____	have caught
2. swim	swam	_____
3. _____	rose	have risen
4. bite	bit	_____
5. dive	_____	have dived (dove)
6. fly	_____	have flown
7. freeze	_____	_____
8. sit	sat	_____
9. hang (execute)	hanged	_____
10. hang (suspend)	_____	have hung
11. drink	drank	_____
12. shake	_____	have shaken
13. _____	shrank	_____
14. _____	spoke	have spoken
15. swear	_____	have sworn
16. _____	grew	_____
17. sink	sank	_____
18. drown	_____	have drowned
19. sing	sang	_____

Can you solve this riddle, using parts of the verbs **lay, lie,** and **lie**?

IF YOU _____ DOWN AND SAY YOU HAVE _____ DOWN, YOU WILL HAVE _____ .

Name _____

SEASIDE SCENES

> A **transitive** verb shows action and is always
>   followed by an object which receives the action.
> An **intransitive** verb does not have an object which
>   receives action.

Example: The whale **swallowed** the diver. *(transitive)*
    The diver **escaped** through the blow hole. *(intransitive)*

Picture each of the following scenes from the sea in your mind.
Mark sentences with a T if they contain a transitive verb
and with an I if they contain an intransitive verb.
Circle the objects of the transitive verbs.

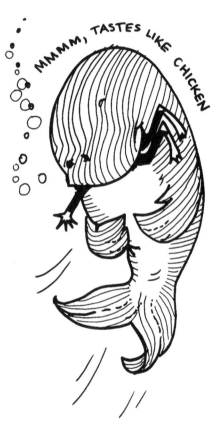

MMMM, TASTES LIKE CHICKEN

_____ 1. Kites fly high over the crystal waters.

_____ 2. Rays float like large pancakes in the shallow waters.

_____ 3. Divers spear fish for a lunch on the beach.

_____ 4. A ship sails west into the sunset.

_____ 5. Waves wash the rocky shoreline.

_____ 6. A mother manatee nurtures her young.

_____ 7. Jet skis play with the waves.

_____ 8. A pilot fish swims alongside a sand shark.

_____ 9. Children gather shells on the sand.

_____ 10. An octopus teases a starfish.

_____ 11. A nervous lifeguard watches five young children in the waves.

_____ 12. Three frightened swimmers avoid large jellyfish.

_____ 13. Sunburned tourists find shade under umbrellas.

_____ 14. Gulls disappear into the clouds.

_____ 15. She sells seashells at the seashore.

Name _____

OBJECT OVERLOAD

Hector is off to the beach, slightly overloaded, wouldn't you say? He's got a few too many beach objects. While he's looking for places to set up all his objects, you can be looking for direct and indirect objects.

> A **direct object** is a noun or pronoun to which the action of a verb is done, answering the question *what?* or *whom?*
> Example: The kids bounced beach balls. (*Balls* is the direct object.)
>
> An **indirect object** is a noun or pronoun that comes between the verb and the direct object. It tells *to whom* or *to what* the action is done.
> Example: Greg threw his friend a beach ball. (*Friend* is the indirect object.)

For each sentence below, underline the object(s). Then, above each one you underline, write **D** for **direct** object or **I** for **indirect** object.

1. Hector needed a wheelbarrow for his trip to the beach.

2. Under the boardwalk, I found shelter from the sun (and from Hector).

3. Unfortunately, Hector found me under the boardwalk.

4. He gave me the job of watching his stuff while he went swimming.

5. Along the way down the beach, he picked up many shells.

6. As he plunged into the water, the waves gave him a beating.

7. Hector had put his faith in his new floating device. (It didn't help him much.)

8. As the lifeguards watched Hector struggle in the surf, he gave them a serious scare.

9. It was two hours before he returned, hollering, "I came to get my stuff."

10. In the meantime, I had loaned a kind old lady his umbrella.

11. It provided her sunburned husband some relief from the sun.

12. I confess, I shared most of the other objects, too.

13. Hector bombarded me with threats and insults for a long, loud time.

14. "Hey, I don't even know this guy," I told amused onlookers.

15. I think I'll find another beach for my next sea visit.

16. Shall I introduce you to Hector?

IT TAKES <u>NO</u> GENIUS TO <u>KNOW</u> THAT I'M FREQUENTLY <u>SEEN</u> AROUND THE BEACH <u>SCENE</u>.

Name

TROUBLESOME VERBS

Do you lie or lay on the beach? Unless you are a hen,
it would probably be more conventional to lie!

> **Lie** (to rest or recline) .... **Lay** (to put or place)
>
> **Sit** (to rest in a seated position) .... **Set** (to place or put something)
>
> **Rise** (to go upward) ..... **Raise** (to make something else go upward)

NOT A BAD LIFE FOR A CHICKEN

I. Circle the correct choice for each sentence.
1. We (lay, laid) on the beach.
2. We (lay, laid) our towels on the beach.
3. We (raised, rose) our awning for shade.
4. While we were (rising, raising) the tent, Josh (sat, set) his radio on the towel.
5. "Don't (lay, lie) those bottles there," hollered the beach patrol.
6. Sue (lay, lied) down on the lounge chair while the rest of us (set, sat) by the pool.
7. Niki got splashed by a dive bomb and (rose, raised) so quickly that she upset a book she had (laid, lain) on the chair, and it fell into the water.
8. "Why didn't I (set, sit) that on the table?" she moaned.
9. Ted was (laying, lying) on a chaise nearby.
10. When he saw the submerged book, he quickly (raised, rose) to the occasion.
11. The smile he got from Niki as he (lay, laid) the book in her hands was his reward.
12. Later, we enjoyed (setting, sitting) on the beach, watching the winds (raise, rise) and fall against the far-off spinnaker sails.

II. Fill in the blank with the form of the verb specified in parentheses.

Rise/Raise
1. The flag will be _____ at sunrise. *(past participle)*
2. The sun _____ slowly over the horizon. *(past tense)*

Lie/Lay
3. The bricks were _____ in a zigzag pattern. *(past participle)*
4. Mike had to _____ on his stomach because his back was burned. *(present tense)*

Sit/Set
5. We were _____ on the deck when lightning struck. *(present participle)*
6. The students _____ on the beach for the concert. *(past tense)*

Name _____

AGREE OR DISAGREE

Deep-sea divers usually get along with most of the sea creatures they meet. If they don't, it could be disastrous. Subjects and verbs in clauses need to get along, too. If they disagree, sentences will sound strange or be confusing.

> The **subject** and **verb** of any clause must **agree in number.** If a subject is singular, the verb must be singular. Example: The lobster's claw *(sing.)* is *(sing.)* dangerous. If a subject is plural, the verb must be plural. Example: Divers *(plural)* dress *(plural)* carefully.

I. Do these subjects and verbs get along? YES or NO? Correct each sentence where the subject and verb do not agree.

_____ 1. Neither Pete nor Doug are going water skiing. _____

_____ 2. Sand fleas are disgusting pests. _____

_____ 3. A gull's favorite meal is not macaroni and cheese. _____

_____ 4. Tracy's pants is blowing overboard. _____

_____ 5. The boys boast broad muscles and big tattoos. _____

_____ 6. Baked peanut butter and moldy cheese makes a cooler stink! _____

_____ 7. Each of the contestants are required to model bathing suits. _____

_____ 8. Half of the drinks was missing. _____

_____ 9. Everybody is invited to the clambake. _____

_____ 10. Lots of singers and dancers is on the program. _____

_____ 11. One of the musicians are doing a comedy act. _____

_____ 12. Where are the bongo players? _____

_____ 13. The group, The Sandpipers, wasn't any good. _____

_____ 14. What if one of the hula dancers trip and falls. _____

II. Match each subject with an agreeable verb.
    (You will need to use only about half the verbs!)

SUBJECTS	VERBS	
geese	hides	surfaces
a submarine	scurry	fly
the sea captain	pinches	honks
angel fish	swim	commands
sand crabs	dive	salute

Name

REEF RIOT

The reef is loaded with sea life. This story about the reef is loaded with adjectives. Adjectives should answer the questions **"How many?" "What kind?"** or **"Which one?"** Identify and circle the adjectives in the story below.

A leisurely, 100-yard swim brought us to the off-shore reef. We were looking for loose shells, unusual coral formations, flowering anemones, and brightly colored fish; we were looking out for sea spines, fire coral, moray eels, and unfriendly sharks. Jason had brought some bread crusts to entice the tiny reef fish, and Jen hoped that her can of cheese curls would attract some of the larger, hungry inhabitants. Dan and Joe had tucked some leftover chum in their pockets, just in case they saw a nosy squid or a scouting ray. Excited by the unexplored wonders of the reef and energized by the cool, clear Caribbean waters, we skimmed along the shallower, in-shore edges of the reef. Jess and I poked contentedly at the buzzing population of colorful creatures hidden in the cracks and crevices of the craggy coral. Jen, Jason, Dan, and Joe had rounded the ocean side of the reef and were out of sight. However, a cloud of chum and crumbs, propelled by voluminous bubbles, churned near the turn in the reef. It appeared to be the detritus of a fracas that was taking place on the other side. Jess and I raced recklessly toward the troubled waters. As we rounded the reef, we discovered a mass of frenzied fish swarming around our friends. On the deep, blue, ocean edge of this frightening scenario circled a dark, foreboding shape . . .

In each blank, add one or more adjectives that describe some of the sights you might have seen on the reef. Try to choose words that draw strong visual images and have not been used in the story.

1. _____ tails   2. _____ rocks   3. _____ shapes
4. _____ body   5. _____ waves   6. _____ eyes
7. _____ creature   8. _____ claws   9. _____ caves
10. _____ surface   11. _____ fish   12. _____ grasses
13. _____ scales   14. _____ teeth   15. _____ coral
16. _____ skies   17. _____ sounds   18. _____ divers

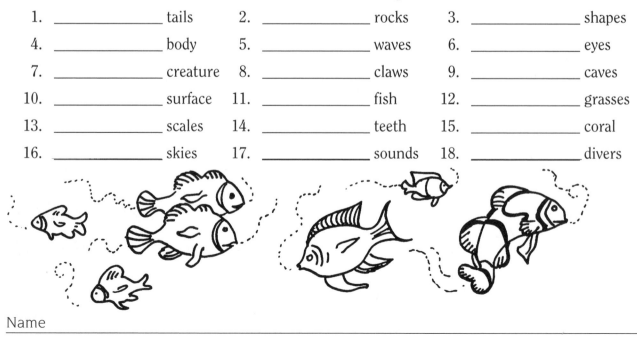

Name

28

"ADD" VERBS

Where is a shark? **When** did it show up? **How** will we escape? **How often** do they come here?
To what extent should they be allowed?

> Remember that an adverb modifies a verb, an adjective, or another adverb.
>   It answers the questions: **Where? When? How? How often? To what extent?**

I. Add to each sentence an adverb that strongly supports the word it modifies.

1. "Please help me!" cried the child _____ .

2. "Watch that broken glass," _____ warned the girl.

3. _____ , she struck at the intruder.

4. _____ , he gained on his opponent.

5. The examination showed he was improving extremely _____ .

6. _____ , Joy ran to tell the good news.

7. A _____ powerful prince presided over the proceedings.

8. _____ , the flight is on time.

9. The concert is _____ sold out.

10. Hoards of bees swarmed _____ around their heads.

11. _____ , I ate a monstrous meal.

12. _____ , a person can find solitude.

II. Write a news story that has at least one adverb in each sentence. Underline the adverbs in your
    story. Circle the words they modify.

SHARK SIGHTING CLOSES BEACHES

WHERE? _____

WHEN? _____

HOW? _____

HOW OFTEN? _____

TO WHAT EXTENT? _____

Name _____

FAST, FASTER, FASTEST

You can't compare the speeds of the boats without using comparatives and superlatives.

> A **comparative adjective** or **adverb** is used to describe a comparison between two things, person, places, or actions.
>
> A **superlative adjective** or **adverb** compares three or more things, persons, places, or actions.

I. Decide whether each word listed below is an adjective or adverb. Then enter it on the appropriate chart and add its comparative and superlative forms.

good	late	happy	easy	happily	easily
badly	many	bad	stubborn	loud	well (how something is done)

ADJECTIVES:

	Positive	Comparative	Superlative
1.	_____	_____	_____
2.	_____	_____	_____
3.	_____	_____	_____
4.	_____	_____	_____
5.	_____	_____	_____
6.	_____	_____	_____
7.	_____	_____	_____
8.	_____	_____	_____

ADVERBS:

	Positive	Comparative	Superlative
1.	_____	_____	_____
2.	_____	_____	_____
3.	_____	_____	_____
4.	_____	_____	_____

II. Fill in each blank with a word that makes the proper comparisons about the picture above, using a form of the word in parentheses.

1. *The Whiz* is slightly _____ than *The Sea Sharp*. (fast)

2. *Mother's Worry* is the _____ boat of the three. (fast)

3. *The Whiz* is _____ to *The Sea Sharp* than to *Mother's Worry*. (near)

4. *The Sea Sharp* is the _____ boat in the race. (big)

5. *Mother's Worry* is the racer _____ to the finish line. (close)

Name _____

NO DANGLING, PLEASE

It's not a good idea to dangle your feet off the pier unless you're sure about what's lurking below the surface of the water. It's also not a good idea to dangle modifiers in sentences.

> When sentences or phrases are combined, the relationship between them must be clear. If a modifying clause or phrase does not clearly and sensibly modify a word in the sentence, or if it is not placed close to the word it modifies, it is called a **dangling modifier.**
>   Crabs were served to the guests *covered with butter.*

See if you can straighten out these danglers by rewriting the sentences correctly.

1. While riding a bicycle, a stray dog bit me.

   _____

2. Jutting out of the sea, the swimmers were shocked to see a fin.

   _____

3. While eating its food, I suddenly noticed how fat our dog was becoming.

   _____

4. Riding horseback along the beach, the ocean looked very peaceful.

   _____

5. Why did you buy saltwater taffy from a store that was unwrapped?

   _____

6. Joe lost the music he had written by mistake.

   _____

7. My mother told me to put on sunscreen at least ten times this week.

   _____

8. I repaired the raft that was punctured by the shark with great care.

   _____

Name _____

A DOUBLE NEGATIVE IS A NO-NO!!

Scuba diving alone is a no-no. So is using double negatives. Never get caught doing either of these!

> A **double negative** is a construction in which two negatives are used when one is sufficient!

Underline the double negatives you find in the following sentences. Then rewrite each of those sentences, correcting the error(s). Several sentences are correct. In the spaces at the bottom of the page, record the first letter of each correct sentence, and your wise choices will reveal a double positive!

1. You have only five minutes of air in your tank.

   _____

2. Tina couldn't hardly move her arm after the jellyfish sting.

   _____

3. Didn't you ever do nothing about that leak in the boat?

   _____

4. Evan can hardly see through his clouded mask.

   _____

5. We haven't but two days of vacation left.

   _____

6. I can't find no shipwrecks around here.

   _____

7. Scuba diving alone makes no sense.

   _____

8. Bob never dives in no dangerous places.

   _____

9. Yesterday, we had scarcely any free time to swim.

   _____

10. There isn't no ice left in the cooler.

    _____

11. Everyone searched for treasure, but there was none.

    _____

12. Seven divers have searched, but haven't found anything.

    _____

13. I haven't ever seen no barracuda.

    _____

14. If you aren't seeing one now, you're not seeing nothing!

    _____

_____ _____ _____ , _____ _____ _____ !

Name _____

POSITIONS, PLEASE!

The little starfish is next to the fat starfish. The skinny starfish is not near the little one. But none of them are inside a predator.

> **Next, near,** and **inside** are prepositions. A **preposition** is a word that shows the relationship of a noun or pronoun to some other word in the sentence.

I. Locate only the prepositions in the following list. Write each preposition in a place on the drawing which illustrates its proper relationship to the drawing. (You may use arrows when necessary.)

around	*above*	*the*	*beside*	*toward*
below	*neither*	*over*	*between*	*after*
on	*nor*	*either*	*across*	*yet*
against	*and*	*through*	*underneath*	*within*
behind	*instead*	*both*	*near*	*you*

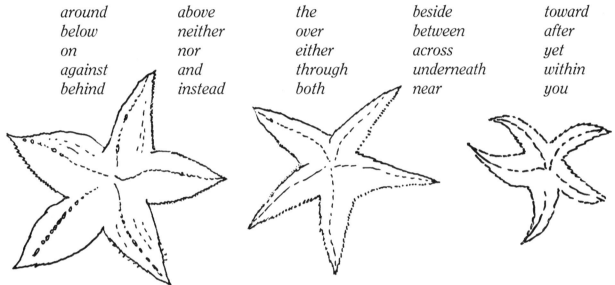

> A **prepositional phrase** is a phrase that begins with a preposition and ends with a noun.

II. Write a prepositional phrase to go with each noun. Use each preposition only once!

1. _____ rickety stairs
2. _____ burning sand
3. _____ a melting igloo
4. _____ a wacky tea party
5. _____ a dancing bear
6. _____ chicken soup
7. _____ crashing waves
8. _____ sticky syrup
9. _____ an ugly octopus
10. _____ two slippery eels

Name _____

A WHALE OF A TALE

This tale about a whale is loaded with participles and participial phrases. (Most tales are!) Can you find them all?

> A **participle** is a verb form that is used as an adjective.
>
> A **present participle** usually consists of the verb plus **ing.**
>
> A **past participle** usually consists of the verb plus **d** or **ed** and occasionally **t, en,** or **n.**

I. Underline the participles in the sentences below.

1. Caught by a storm, a large whale was washed ashore by the waves.

2. Jumping up and down with delight, the children gathered around the beached animal.

3. The mammal, given the right care, could be saved.

4. The marine biologists worked carefully, keeping the animal wet as they examined it.

5. Encouraged by the crowd, the whale was able to return to his ocean home.

6. Moving out to sea, he tipped his tail to his landlubber friends.

7. Pleased with their accomplishment, the crowd cheered.

> A **participial phrase** is the participle and its related words, acting together as an adjective.

II. Fill each space below with a participial phrase.

1. The whale _____ was a female.

2. The waves _____ were complicating the rescue efforts.

3. _____ , the whale finally got turned around.

4. The rescuers, _____ , were able to coax the whale forward.

5. _____ , the children waved joyfully as the whale swam out to sea.

6. The people, _____ , cheered the rescuers.

7. _____ , everyone made his way home happily.

Name _____

JUGGLING GERUNDS

Swimming, diving, snorkeling, burning, screaming, chasing—these are some of the many gerunds you might find at the beach.

> A **gerund** is a verb form, ending in **ing**, that is used as a **noun.**
> Like nouns, gerunds can be used as **subjects, predicate nominatives, direct** or **indirect objects,** or **objects of prepositions.**

I. Circle the gerund in each sentence; then, on the line provided, tell how it is used.

1. Juggling on water skis is a nearly impossible feat.

2. I like jet skiing better.

3. At the point of breaking, waves are most powerful.

4. Body surfing can be dangerous.

5. The most popular beach sport is watching people.

6. The girls gave sunning most of their time and energy.

7. The boys loved playing volleyball.

8. Are there any rules for boating here?

9. I have lain here all day and given my reading not one thought.

10. A rocking boat makes taking pictures difficult.

> A **gerund phrase** is a gerund with all of its related words, acting together as a noun.

II. Write a gerund phrase to complete each sentence below.

1. _____ is a difficult task.

2. Most kids love _____ .

3. _____ seemed to excite the fish.

4. The problem _____ was one we had to solve quickly.

Name _____

TO SWIM IS TO SURVIVE

The title of this page has two infinitives. This sentence has two more: "If this swimmer is going to live through the day, she needs to make it to the island." Can you find them?

An **infinitive** is a verb form, usually preceded by the word **to.** It may be used as a **noun, adjective,** or **adverb.**

I. Circle the infinitives in the sentences below.

1. I love to eat clams.
2. To locate one tiny boat on the ocean is difficult.
3. We hope to sail to Bimini this winter.
4. The captain seemed to be ill.
5. The motor sounds as if it is about to quit.
6. To swim is to survive.

An **infinitive phrase** is an infinitive together with all of its related words.

II. For each picture below, write a sentence that includes an infinitive phrase.

1. _____

2. _____

3. _____

4. _____

Name _____

LONERS AND LEANERS

"If you are alone, you can lean on me!!"

  (dependent)   (independent)

An **independent clause** expresses a complete thought and can stand by itself. (It's a LONER!)

A **dependent (subordinate) clause** does **not** express a complete thought and **cannot** stand alone. (It's a LEANER!)

Choose from the following list of "loners" and "leaners" five pairs of clauses that can be used to create five sentences. Write your sentences on the lines below. Each sentence should contain one independent and one subordinate clause.

after he had swallowed a gold ring	he fell off the dock
while he was changing	after he kissed her
when my family vacationed in Bermuda	they witnessed a drowning
while she was cleaning his fish	the fish was so big
his pants blew away	that I will never forget it
his date fainted	a giant sea turtle washed ashore

1. _____

   _____

2. _____

   _____

3. _____

   _____

4. _____

   _____

5. _____

   _____

Name _____

CLAUSE CAUGHT IN CLAWS???

Don't get caught in confusion about clauses. Practice finding clauses that **depend** on others.

A **dependent clause** is a group of words that has a subject and predicate but does not express a complete thought. It **depends** on an **independent clause** to complete its meaning.

Underline the dependent clause in each sentence. Then, in the numbered space, tell whether it is used as a noun, adjective, or adverb.

_____ 1. The lobster who had the biggest claws won the fight.

_____ 2. The fish that Meg caught was 21 inches long.

_____ 3. Before the sun was up, we had our equipment ready.

_____ 4. Yvette, who has been fishing since she was a child, won the contest.

_____ 5. That big barracuda knows what our fishing secrets are.

_____ 6. Because he felt seasick, Kirk hung over the stern.

_____ 7. Here is the pole for which you have been looking.

_____ 8. Whoever wins the battle gets a date with a mermaid.

_____ 9. After we had fished all day, we got dressed up for dinner and dancing.

_____ 10. We often dream that we live in an underwater castle.

_____ 11. When that happens, we usually have just fallen asleep in the bathtub!

_____ 12. Who knows what the future will bring?

_____ 13. We may be living in an underwater kingdom where everything is peaceful.

_____ 14. If you should find a genie in a bottle at sea, what three wishes would you ask for?

Name _____

COOL OR OBTUSE???

Cal, the lifeguard, gave himself the name Cool Cal. He thinks he is cool for many reasons. One of them is that he's a whiz at capitalization—or so he thinks! If Cal has correctly capitalized an item below, give it a C (for COOL); if it is incorrect, give it an O (for OBTUSE). If you don't know the meaning of the word *obtuse*, look it up. Then transform the Os to COOL by making proper corrections.

_____ 1. a small Catholic church on Shelby Avenue

_____ 2. fingerprints taken by officer Wiley

_____ 3. You'll love victorian literature!

_____ 4. See you on Labor Day!

_____ 5. the Washington monument

_____ 6. We visited the great Smoky mountains.

_____ 7. My high school teacher went to Duke University.

_____ 8. traveling East on U.S. I-40

_____ 9. my father's sister, Cleopatra

_____ 10. buddhists worship in temples

_____ 11. I hope she won't tell mom!

_____ 12. He went to the Southwest to school.

_____ 13. American red cross

_____ 14. I flunked Spanish, but I passed chemistry.

_____ 15. the Canadians won the gold medal!

_____ 16. I've read the holy bible, cover to cover.

_____ 17. I love new England in the fall.

_____ 18. Welcome to the senior Class Picnic.

_____ 19. He drives a red pickup truck.

_____ 20. He drives a Mighty Man Brand truck.

Name _____

CLEARLY CLOUDY

I. Correct the errors in punctuation and capitalization on this envelope and business letter.

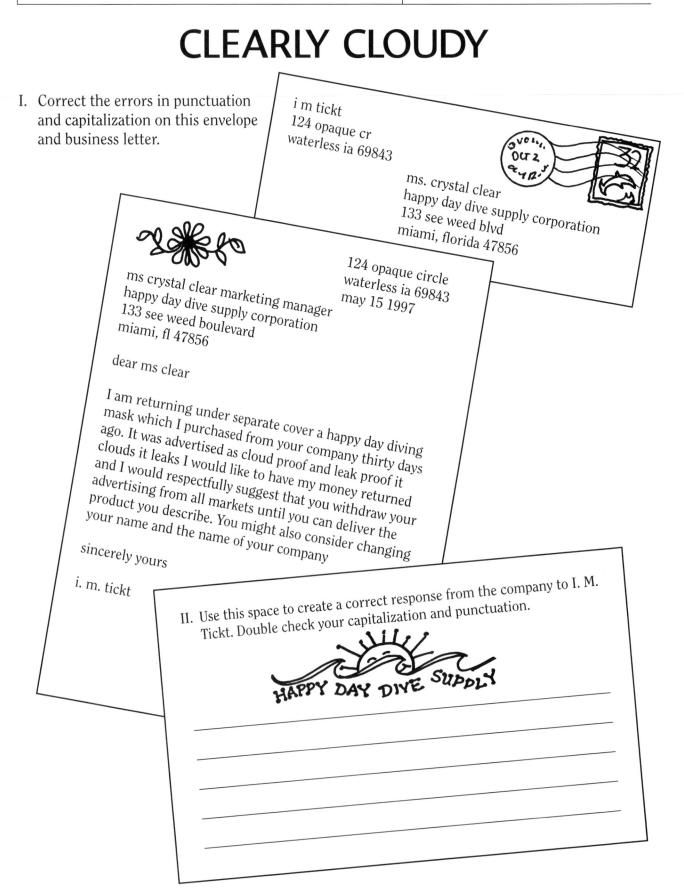

i m tickt
124 opaque cr
waterless ia 69843

ms. crystal clear
happy day dive supply corporation
133 see weed blvd
miami, florida 47856

124 opaque circle
waterless ia 69843
may 15 1997

ms crystal clear marketing manager
happy day dive supply corporation
133 see weed boulevard
miami, fl 47856

dear ms clear

I am returning under separate cover a happy day diving mask which I purchased from your company thirty days ago. It was advertised as cloud proof and leak proof it clouds it leaks I would like to have my money returned and I would respectfully suggest that you withdraw your advertising from all markets until you can deliver the product you describe. You might also consider changing your name and the name of your company

sincerely yours

i. m. tickt

II. Use this space to create a correct response from the company to I. M. Tickt. Double check your capitalization and punctuation.

HAPPY DAY DIVE SUPPLY

TITLE-WISE

When you're reading a good book or magazine at the beach, you don't have to worry about its title—at least not after you've picked the one you're going to read. But when you write titles, it gets a little tricky, and you need to know the rules.

Titles of books, plays, movies, periodicals, works of art, long musical compositions, and book-length poems are underlined or written in italics.

Titles of magazine articles, short stories, poems, songs, chapters, and other parts of books or periodicals are enclosed in quotation marks.

Capitalize the first letter in the first and last words as well as in nouns, verbs, adverbs, adjectives, and pronouns in titles. Do not capitalize prepositions, articles, or conjunctions.

Write at least two appropriate titles (real ones) for each category below. Use reference materials if you need help in identifying real titles.

CITY NEWSPAPERS _____

FAMOUS WORKS OF ART _____

BOOKS _____

SONGS _____

PERIODICALS _____

SHORT STORIES _____

SHORT POEMS _____

MOVIES _____

CHAPTER TITLES _____

MAGAZINE ARTICLES _____

Name _____

PUNCTUATION REPAIR

Some of the signs in this town are in need of repair. Fix each sign by adding needed punctuation or by crossing out marks used in error.

YES WE HAVE NO BANANAS
COME AND GET EM

LOBSTER
1-3 LBS

DONUT HOLE'S BAGELS
COFFEE AND CROISSANTS

DEW DROP INN
TIRED DROP HERE

BOSTON MASSACHUSETTS
107 MI

THE BICYCLE DOCTOR
JOE WHEELER JR
FIX IT IN A MINUTE

POSITIVELY!
NO FISHING

BOATS AND JET SKI'S
FOR RENT
OPEN 7AM–6PM

Oh, oh . . . a lost letter has been blown into the street. It needs a good editor, too!

dear Jose
Its christmas where are you weve called and called please get in touch we miss you worried maria

Name

A PERFECT DAY FOR DIVING

This is the story of seven snorkelers going off to take advantage of a perfect day. But the story is a mess. It's in need of a proofreader—that's you! Use proofreaders' marks to make the necessary insertions and corrections in capitalization and punctuation on the copy below. Then use the rest of the page to rewrite the story. If you need more space, use the back of the page.

---

the day was clear and calm extraordinary for off shore diving we packed wet suits towels masks snorkels flippers soft drinks and chips and threw in some squeeze cheese for the fish

last man into the trucks a flat flounder yelled jed

Oh no whered I put my new watch it was waterproof and had a luminous dial I got it 'specially for diving

honk

coming yes there it is OK

I jammed my super sharks baseball cap onto my head

a moment later seven of us were crammed into the 4 X 4 headed to the emerald waters of eden rock off to coral reefs caves and fluorescent fish maybe wed see a ray or a barracuda or a sand shark maybe wed tease a fat old moray eel out of his cave

adventure here we come

A PERFECT DAY FOR DIVING

_____

_____

_____

_____

_____

_____

_____

_____

LOST IN THE WAVES

This tale has gotten caught up in a big wave. Unfortunately, all the commas have been lost. Find all the places where commas have been washed away. Use a colored pen or pencil to insert them where they belong.

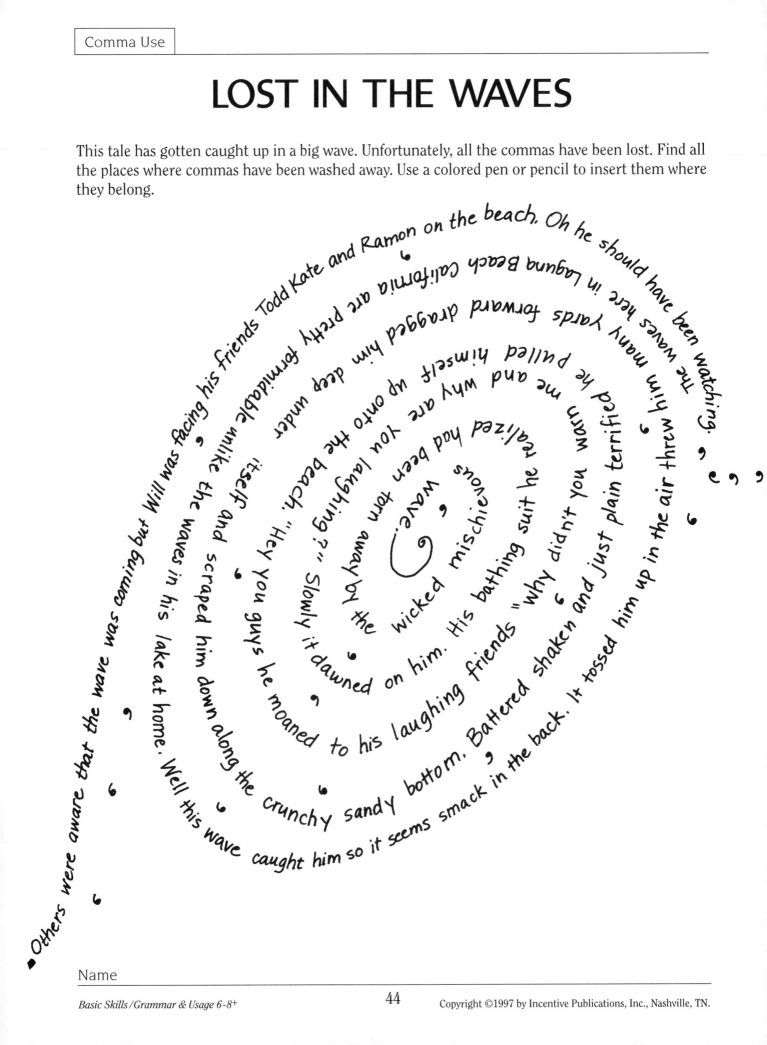

The spiraling text reads: Will was facing his friends Todd, Kate, and Ramon on the beach. Oh, he should have been watching. The waves here in Laguna Beach, California, are pretty formidable unlike the waves in his lake at home. Well, this wave caught him so it seems, dragged him deep under, scraped him down along the crunchy, sandy bottom. Battered, shaken, and just plain terrified, he pulled himself up onto the beach. "Hey, you guys," he moaned to his laughing friends, "why didn't you warn me and why are you laughing?" Slowly it dawned on him. His bathing suit he realized had been torn away by the wicked, mischievous wave. It tossed him up in the air, threw him many yards forward. Others were aware that the wave was coming but Will was not.

QUOTABLES

Old Carlotta Crocodile says that if you should meet a crocodile, you should not take a stick and poke him. (This is an indirect quote.) See the direct quote below.

I. The sentences below contain indirect quotations. Rewrite each sentence, changing the quote to a direct quotation, correctly punctuated.

1. Mark Twain once said that a lie can travel halfway around the world while the truth is putting on its shoes.

   _____

   _____

2. You will probably agree with Roger Lewin's observation that, too often, we give children answers to remember rather than problems to solve.

   _____

   _____

3. Do you know what H. G. Wells meant when he proposed that civilization is a race between education and catastrophe?

   _____

   _____

4. Thomas Jefferson stated that he was a great believer in luck and found that the harder he worked, the more he had of it.

   _____

   _____

5. Will Rogers says everybody is ignorant, only on different subjects!

   _____

   _____

II. Punctuate these sentences:
   1. Look cried Louis its a rainbow
   2. I can hardly wait chattered Benita Tomorrow is my birthday
   3. Do you know how old I'll be she asked Thirteen—a real teenager

Name _____

COLON & COMPANY

Detective Inspector Sharpeye, disguised as a beach bum, is lurking around tracking down missing colons and semicolons. He's hoping for your help.

The slash mark in each item below means a colon or semicolon may be missing from that space. Your mission, should you decide to accept it, is to discover which sentence in each pair needs a colon or a semicolon. Indicate your choice (A or B) on the lines to the right, and mark the correct punctuation in the sentence that is missing a colon or semicolon.

1. A. The ship sails at 7 / 37 P.M.
   B. The train leaves at a quarter after / midnight.   1. _____

2. A. Sincerely /
   B. To Whom It May Concern /   2. _____

3. A. The train stopped / the passengers poured out.
   B. The children were sent / to clean up their mess.   3. _____

4. A. The party was so crowded / that there was no room to dance.
   B. The tide came in / most of the swimmers left the beach.   4. _____

5. A. The curtain fell / when the orchestra finished the concert.
   B. His new record album is terrific / it'll go gold.   5. _____

6. A. Gentlemen /
   B. Sincerely yours /   6. _____

7. A. The following items are not allowed on the beach / glass,
      pets, and rafts.
   B. The museum exhibited the works of / Monet, Manet,
      and Renoir.   7. _____

8. A. The wedding day ended / as happily as it began.
   B. The kids made the dinner / the parents did the dishes.   8. _____

9. A. The Beach Boys toured / Europe, Asia, and Australia.
   B. We couldn't get tickets / the tour was sold out.   9. _____

10. A. Stop flapping about / like a two-ton flipper.
    B. Stay away from me / you're getting me wet!   10. _____

11. A. They should put up a sign that says / bugs aren't allowed.
    B. Three things are bugging me / mosquitoes, ants, and fleas.   11. _____

12. A. Doug broke his nose / and is on crutches.
    B. Crutches are silly / it's his nose, not his knee.   12. _____

Name _____

BRILLIANT DEVICES

The **dash**, the **hyphen**, and **parentheses** are all brilliant devices to help you write interesting sentences. Check your grammar handbook or textbook to review the purposes and rules for using these devices. Then insert them properly in the examples below.

THE DRAMATIC DASH

1. The boss raged into the office, screamed obscenities at his staff and his pants fell to his knees.

2. The vicar's knickers are thicker and slicker a clever rhyme.

3. Aunt Prunella had a face that matched her personality pinched, pink, and powdery.

4. One hundred-year-old George Galguggener swims eight miles a day an amazing feat!

THE HEROIC HYPHEN

5. He raged into the office and screamed at his staff in obscenity laden language.

6. A mad dog debriefed the vicar, making him the ex knickered vicar.

7. Aunt Prunella is the seventy six year old mother in law of president elect, Peter Papagallo.

8. Mr. Galguggener, a one hundred year old ex marine frogman, says he can swim forty six miles a week.

THE PERIPATETIC PARENTHESES

9. When the boss screamed, his pants fell down. I think he popped his belt.

10. The vicar appeared at the beach in a pair of neon knickers. What a nerd!

11. Aunt Prunella was the descendant and, of course, namesake of the great Prosperpina Prunella Piccadilly Pepperdine.

12. The oldest swimmer in town he claims to be one hundred swims eight miles every day.

Name

SAILORS' NOTS

Sailors use very clever, secure knots to tie two things together. **Contractions** are like knots. They tie words together in a shortened or combined form. An **apostrophe** shows where letters have been left out when the knot is tied!

I. In each of the knots below, "tie" the pair of words together to create a contraction.

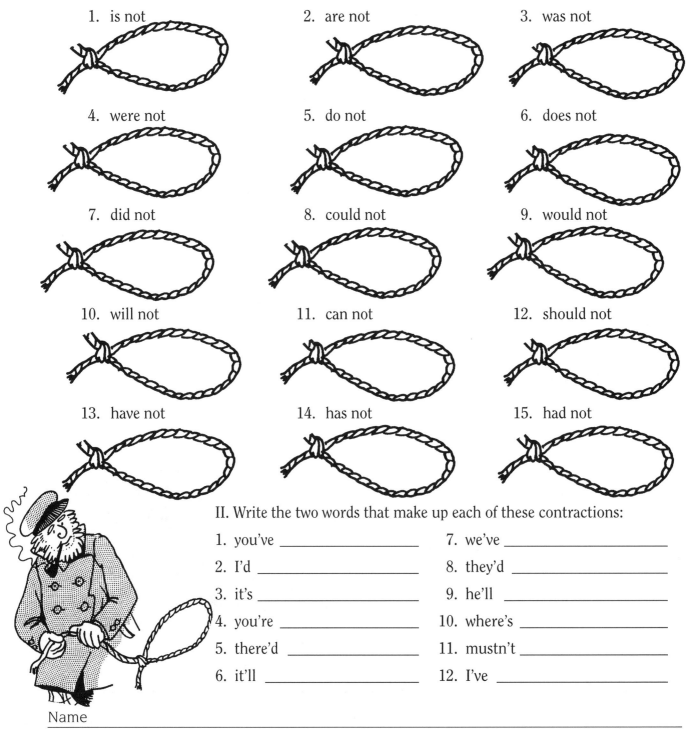

1. is not
2. are not
3. was not

4. were not
5. do not
6. does not

7. did not
8. could not
9. would not

10. will not
11. can not
12. should not

13. have not
14. has not
15. had not

II. Write the two words that make up each of these contractions:

1. you've _____
2. I'd _____
3. it's _____
4. you're _____
5. there'd _____
6. it'll _____

7. we've _____
8. they'd _____
9. he'll _____
10. where's _____
11. mustn't _____
12. I've _____

Name _____

APPENDIX

CONTENTS

CAPITALIZATION AND PUNCTUATION GUIDE

CAPITALIZE:

- the first word of every sentence
- the first word in a direct quotation
- all proper nouns and proper adjectives
- the first word in the greeting and closing of a letter
- names of people and also the initials or abbreviations that stand for those names
- titles used with names of persons and abbreviations standing for those titles
- geographical names and sections of the country or world
- names of languages, races, nationalities, religions, and proper adjectives formed from them
- names of days of the week, months of the year, and special holidays
- names of historical events, documents, and periods of time
- names of organizations, associations, teams, and their members
- abbreviations of titles and organizations
- names of businesses and official names of their products
- the first letter of the first, last, and other important words in a title
- words such as *mother, father, aunt,* and *uncle* when these words are used as names

Punctuate with a PERIOD:

- to end a declarative sentence
- to end an imperative sentence that is not an exclamation
- after an initial
- after each part of an abbreviation, unless the abbreviation is an acronym (When an abbreviation is the last word in the sentence, use only one period.)
- after numbers and letters in outlines
- as a decimal point and to separate dollars and cents

Punctuate with an ELLIPSIS:

- for a pause in dialogue
- to show that one or more words are left out of a quotation
- when the final words are left out of a sentence (Ellipsis is placed after the period.)

Punctuate with a COMMA:

- to separate words, phrases, or clauses in a series (at least three items)

- in a quotation, to set off the exact words of a speaker from the rest of the sentence
- after the greeting and closing in an informal letter
- to separate the month and day from the year in a date
- to separate the names of a city and state in an address
- to separate a noun of direct address from the rest of the sentence
- to separate an interjection or weak exclamation from the rest of the sentence
- to separate two or more adjectives which modify the same noun
- to set off a word, phrase, or clause that interrupts the main thought of a sentence
- to separate an appositive or other explanatory phrase from the rest of the sentence
- to enclose a title, name, or initials which follow a person's last name
- between two independent clauses joined by such words as: *but, or, for, so, yet*
- to separate a long modifying phrase from the independent clause which follows it
- to punctuate nonrestrictive phrases (a nonrestrictive phrase or clause is not necessary to the basic meaning of the sentence)
- to separate digits in a number to set apart places of hundreds, thousands, millions, etc.
- whenever necessary to make meaning clear

Punctuate with a SEMICOLON:

- to separate groups of words or phrases which already contain commas
  (We visited beaches in Miami, Florida; Malibu, California; Maui, Hawaii; and Bandon, Oregon.)
- to connect two independent clauses which are not connected with a coordinate conjunction
  (I shared my lunch with a crab; it wasn't a good idea.)
- to connect two independent clauses when the second clause begins with a conjunctive adverb
  such as: *also, as a result, for example, however, therefore*
  (The weather was terrible; therefore we canceled our sailing trip.)

Punctuate with a COLON:

- after the greeting of a formal letter
- between the parts of a number which indicate time
- to introduce a sentence, question, or quotation *(This is what she shouted: "Save the whales!")*
- to introduce a list *(He carried these things to the beach: an umbrella, two towels, a camera, a chair, and a radio.)*

Punctuate with a DASH:

- to indicate a sudden break or change in the sentence
- to emphasize a word, series of words, phrase, or clause
- to indicate a parenthetical or explanatory phrase or clause
- to use between numbers in a page reference

Punctuate with a HYPHEN:

- to join parts of compound words
- to join the words in compound numbers from twenty-one to ninety-nine
- to divide a word when you run out of room at the end of a line (divide only between syllables)
- to form new words beginning with the prefixes *self, ex, all,* and *great*

Punctuate with PARENTHESES:

- around words which are included in a sentence to add information or help make an idea clearer
- to enclose a question mark after a date or statement to show doubt
- to enclose an author's insertion or comment

Punctuate with a QUESTION MARK:

- at the end of a direct question (an interrogative sentence)
- inside parentheses after a date or statement to show doubt

Punctuate with an EXCLAMATION POINT:

- at the end of an exclamatory sentence
- after a word or phrase to express strong feeling

Punctuate with QUOTATION MARKS:

- before and after direct quotations, placed around exact words quoted
- to punctuate titles of songs, poems, short stories, lectures, courses, episodes of radio or television programs, chapters of books, and articles found in magazines, newspapers, or encyclopedias

Punctuate with UNDERLINING or ITALICS:

- to emphasize words and phrases
- to indicate titles of magazines, newspapers, pamphlets, books, plays, films, radio and TV programs, book-length poems, music albums, names of ships and aircraft, etc.
- to indicate scientific names, foreign words, and any other word, number, or letter being used in a special way

Punctuate with an APOSTROPHE:

- to form the possessive of a noun
- to form the plural of a letter, number, symbol, or a word discussed as a word
- to show that one or more letters have been left out of a word to form a contraction

GRAMMAR & USAGE GUIDE
SENTENCES

TYPES OF SENTENCES

A **sentence** is made up of one or more words which express a complete thought.

A **declarative sentence** makes a statement. It tells something about a person, place, thing, or idea.

An **interrogative sentence** asks a question.

An **imperative sentence** makes a command or a request and often ends in a period (often contains understood subject: you.).

An **exclamatory sentence** communicates strong emotion or surprise.

A **simple sentence** has only one independent clause. It expresses a complete thought. *(Sharks bite.)*

A **compound sentence** is made up of two or more simple sentences. *(Sharks bite, so they should be avoided.)*

A **complex sentence** is made up of one independent clause and one or more dependent clauses. *(Sharks may bite when they are provoked.)*

A **compound-complex sentence** is made up of two or more independent clauses and one or more dependent clauses. *(Divers search shipwrecks and snorkelers explore the reef whenever the water is calm.)*

SENTENCE PARTS

modifier—a word or group of words which changes or adds to the meaning of another word (*frightful* octopus)

subject—the part of a sentence which is doing something or about which something is said (*The experienced lifeguard* races into the water.)

simple subject—the subject without the words which describe or modify it *(lifeguard)*

complete subject—the simple subject and all the words which modify it *(the experienced lifeguard)*

compound subject—made up of two or more simple subjects (*Ice cream and hot dogs* taste great at the beach.)

predicate—the part of the sentence which says something about the subject (Fierce storms *blow wildly across the water.*)

simple predicate—the predicate (verb) without the words which describe or modify it *(blow)*

complete predicate—the simple predicate and all the words which modify or explain it *(blow wildly across the water)*

compound predicate—composed of two or more simple predicates (Fierce storms *blow* wildly and *whip* the water into waves.)

phrase—a group of related words which lacks either a subject or a predicate (or both) *(swim three miles, with a bad sunburn, watching the sun set, terribly hungry)*

clause—a group of related words which has both a subject and a predicate

independent clause—presents a complete thought and can stand as a sentence (*A killer whale can do tricks* when it has been well trained.)

dependent clause—does not present a complete thought and cannot stand as a sentence (A killer whale can do tricks *when it has been well trained.*)

Basic Skills/Grammar & Usage 6-8+

PARTS OF SPEECH

NOUNS

A **noun** is a word which is the name of a person, place, thing, or idea.

proper noun—the name of a specific person, place, thing, or idea

common noun—any noun which does not name a specific person, place, thing, or idea

concrete noun—names a thing that is tangible or physical (can be touched or seen)

abstract noun—names something you can think about but cannot see or touch (*honesty, fear*)

singular noun—names one person, place, thing, or idea

plural noun—names more than one person, place, thing, or idea

nominative case—when the noun is used as the subject of the verb (The *ocean* is blue.)

possessive case—when the noun shows possession or ownership (The *ocean's* color is blue.)

objective case—when the noun is used as the direct object, the indirect object, or the object of the preposition (You'll love the *ocean*.)

noun clause—subordinate clause which functions as a noun (You can swim *wherever you want*.)

PRONOUNS

A **pronoun** is a word used in place of a noun.

personal pronouns—include *I, you, he, she, it, we, they, his, hers, her, its, me, myself, us, yours,* and so on

singular personal pronouns—include *I, you, he, she, it*

plural personal pronouns—include *we, you, they*

first person pronoun—used in place of the name of the speaker (*I* can't swim.)

second person pronoun—used to name the person or thing spoken to (Are *you* a swimmer?)

third person pronoun—used to name the person or thing spoken about (Isn't *she* eating sand?)

nominative case—when the pronoun is used as the subject of the verb. (*You* dive really well.)

possessive case—when the pronoun shows possession or ownership (This beach towel is *mine*.)

objective case—when the pronoun is used as the direct object, indirect object, or object of a preposition (The waves engulfed *me*.)

reflexive pronoun—when a personal pronoun throws the action back upon the subject of a sentence (I gave *myself* a present.)

intensive pronoun—when a personal pronoun calls special attention to a noun or pronoun, giving it special emphasis (Anne *herself* chose the food for this picnic.)

relative pronoun—relates one part of a sentence to a noun or pronoun in another part of the sentence (*who, what, which, that, whoever, whosoever, whatever, whatsoever, whichever*).

indefinite pronoun—does not specifically name its antecedent (the noun or pronoun it replaces) (*Somebody* took my towel.)

interrogative pronoun—asks a question (*Who* is swimming out that far?)

demonstrative pronoun—points out a noun (*That* is a dangerous habit!)

VERBS

A **verb** is a word which expresses action or existence.

Verb phrase—includes a main verb and one or more helping verbs *(is swimming, has gone)*

singular verb—a verb with a singular subject (The diver *scores* a perfect 10.)

plural verb—a verb with a plural subject (The divers *score* a perfect 10.)

first person verb—agrees with *I, us, we*

second person verb—agrees with *you*

third person verb—agrees with *he, she, it, they,* proper names, etc.

active voice verb—used when the subject is doing the action in a sentence (Jana *sails* well.)

passive voice verb—if the subject is receiving the action or not doing the action himself (Jana *was taken* on a sailing trip.)

present tense—when a verb expresses action which is happening now or which happens continually (I *choose* this spot for the beach party.)

past tense—when a verb expresses action which is completed at a particular time in the past (I *chose* this spot for the beach party.)

future tense—when a verb expresses action that will take place (I *will choose* this spot.)

present perfect tense—when a verb expresses action that took place in the past and may still be going on (I *have chosen* this spot.)

past perfect tense—when a verb expresses action which began in the past and was completed in the past (I wish I *had chosen* this spot for the beach party.)

future perfect tense—when a verb expresses action or existence which will begin and will be completed by a specific time in the future (I *will have chosen* the spot by tomorrow.)

helping verb—helps to form some of the tenses and voice of the main verb *(was, were, has, have, should have, would have, had been, etc.)*

transitive verb—transfers their action to an object (Doug *bought* a kite.)

direct object—receives the action directly from the subject (Doug bought a *kite.*)

indirect object—receives the action indirectly from the subject (Doug gave his *girlfriend* the kite.)

intransitive verb—completes its action without an object (The boy *fell* from the boat.)

linking verb—an intransitive verb that does not express an action but links a subject to a noun or adjective in the predicate *(is, am, are, were, smell, look, taste, feel, seem, appear . . .)*

verbal—word that is formed from a verb part and used as a noun

gerund—a verb form which ends in *ing* and is used as a noun (*Surfing* is fun.)

gerund phrase—a gerund plus an adjective, adverb, direct object, or preposition (I love *sailing into the wind.*)

infinitive—a verb form usually introduced by *to* (She loves *to surf.*)

infinitive phrase—infinitive plus words that complete its meaning. (It's wise *to surf with care.*)

participle—a verb form ending in *ing* or *ed* used as an adjective (The *laughing* surfers look tired.)

participial phrase—participle and the accompanying words that complete its meaning (*Catching the biggest wave of the day*, he eased up on his surfboard.)

55

ADJECTIVES

An **adjective** is a word used to describe a noun or pronoun (Usually tells **which, what kind,** or **how many.**)

proper adjective—formed from a proper noun and always capitalized

common adjective—any adjective which is not proper

demonstrative adjective—points out a particular noun (*that* scuba gear)

indefinite adjective—gives an approximate number or quantity (*some* suntan lotion)

predicate adjective—follows a linking verb and describes the subject (Those crabs are *busy*.)

positive form—describes a noun or pronoun without comparing it to anything *(tasty)*

comparative form—compares two persons, places, things, or ideas *(tastier)*

superlative form—compares three or more persons, places, things, or ideas *(tastiest)*

adjective clause—a subordinate clause that modifies a noun or a pronoun (We need a lifeguard *that can swim well.*)

ADVERBS

An **adverb** modifies a verb, an adjective, or another adverb. Adverbs are grouped by:
    time—adverbs telling when, how often, how long *(tomorrow, never, often)*
    place—adverbs telling where, to where, or from where *(here, there, inside, under)*
    manner—adverbs telling how something is done *(carefully, well, fast, loudly)*
    degree—adverbs telling how much or how little *(entirely, scarcely, little, totally)*

positive form—describes without comparing to anything *(soon)*

comparative form—compares two verbs, adjectives, or other adverbs *(sooner)*

superlative form—compares more than two verbs, adjectives, or other adverbs *(soonest)*

adverbial clause—a subordinate clause used as an adverb (*Even though it is cloudy,* you can get a sunburn.)

PREPOSITIONS

A **preposition** is a word (or group of words) which shows how two words or ideas are related to each other. A preposition shows the relationship between its object and some other word in the sentence. *(under, in, at, up, on, outside, within, till, over, with)*

A **prepositional phrase** includes the preposition, the object of the preposition, and the modifiers of the object. (It's wise to swim *within sight of the lifeguard.*)

CONJUNCTIONS

A **conjunction** connects individual words or groups of words. *(and, nor, yet, but, or, either, also, although, whereas)*

INTERJECTIONS

An **interjection** is a word or short phrase included in a sentence in order to communicate strong emotion or surprise. An exclamation point is usually used to separate an interjection from the rest of the sentence. *(Wow! Oh! Help!)*

GRAMMAR & USAGE
SKILLS TEST

Use these sentences to answer 1–5.
  A. Knowing it might be dangerous, we took a chance and swam at the pier.
  B. We took a chance, and, oh, were we sorry!
  C. We took our chances.

  1. Which is a simple sentence? _____

  2. Which is a compound sentence? _____

  3. Which is a complex sentence? _____

  4. What's the simple subject of **A?** _____

  5. What's the simple predicate of **C?** _____

Use these sentences to answer 6–11.
  D. Don't swim too near the reef!   **G. Sharks terrify me to death.**
  E. Have you ever actually seen a shark?   **H. Don't be such a chicken.**
  F. Watch for the divers.   **I. Help, that huge shark is after me!**

  6. Which sentence(s) is/are declarative? _____

  7. Which sentence(s) is/are interrogative? _____

  8. Which sentence(s) is/are imperative? _____

  9. Which sentence(s) is/are exclamatory? _____

 10. What is the understood subject of **H?** _____

 11. What is the complete predicate of **G?** _____

For sentences 12–15 below, write **C** for **complete,** **F** for **fragment,** or **R** for **run-on.**

_____ 12. Maria stayed inside all day she had a terrible sunburn.

_____ 13. Because of her severe sunburn.

_____ 14. Feeling miserable, Marie stayed inside all day.

_____ 15. Never having been burned so badly before.

_____ 16. Write the singular form of **mice.**

_____ 17. Write the plural form of **mother-in-law.**

_____ 18. Write the plural form of **beach.**

_____ 19. Write the plural form of **hero.**

_____ 20. Write the possessive meaning **goggles belonging to the swimmer.**

_____ 21. Write the possessive meaning **raft belonging to Jess.**

_____ 22. Write the possessive meaning **the appetites of the lifeguards.**

Name _____

Basic Skills/Grammar & Usage 6-8+

Use these sentences to answer 23-25.
  A. Janelle could feel the tension in the rope from the boat pulling her up on the water skis.
  B. The Walters family loved spending their vacations at Lake Tahoe.
  C. "Who will ski it with me today?" she wondered.

23. Write all the common nouns in **A-C**. _____

24. Write all the proper nouns in **A-C**. _____

25. Write all the pronouns in **A-C**. _____

For 26–37, tell what part of speech each word is as used in sentence **A** or **B**.
  A. The yellow lights from the buoys flashed regularly throughout the night.
  B. Seventeen lighthouse keepers snored loudly every night.

26. yellow _____	30. regularly _____	34. snored _____
27. lights _____	31. throughout _____	35. loudly _____
28. buoys _____	32. lighthouse _____	36. every _____
29. flashed _____	33. keepers _____	37. night _____

Give the past tense and past participle of each of these irregular verbs:

	past	past participle
38. become	_____	_____
39. say	_____	_____
40. do	_____	_____

The lobster pinches! Write the verb in these tenses:

___pinches___ present tense	43. _____ present perfect tense
41. _____ past tense	44. _____ past perfect tense
42. _____ future tense	45. _____ future perfect tense

Circle the correct word for each sentence.
46. Did Dana or Rachael forget (her, their) raft?
47. The beach shop has raised (their, its) prices.
48. Fish and toddlers (eat, eats) worms.
49. His large claws (give, gives) the crab a bad reputation.
50. In the ocean today (are, is) many whales.
51. The teenagers (lay, laid) down their towel.
52. A mother seal came to (lie, lay) on the rock.
53. Don't (sit, set) your glasses on the sand.
54. Six lifeguards suddenly (raised, rose) up and ran to the water.
55. (Who, Whom) will get me some sunscreen?
56. (Who's, Whose) first to get in the water?
57. She's an awesome diver (who, whom) everyone admires.
58. The octopus is the (scary, scarier, scariest) of all the sea animals.
59. I'm a bad diver, but my brother is (worst, worse).
60. Chad's dune buggy can make it over the dunes (easily, more easily, most easily) than I could climb.

Name _____

Tell whether the verb in sentences 61–64 is transitive (T) or intransitive (I).

_____ 61. Speedboats raced throughout the bay.

_____ 62. The lifeguard watched the swimmers.

_____ 63. Surfers lined up along the beach.

_____ 64. A strong undertow caused danger.

65. Which sentences below have a dangling modifier? _____
    A. **Anne filmed fish holding her underwater camera.**
    B. **Hoping for a great wave, her surfboard was ready to go.**
    C. **While waiting for the storm to pass, Jeff hid his boat in a cove.**
    D. **While floating on my raft, a jellyfish stung me.**

66. Which sentences below show correct use of negatives? _____
    E. **There aren't no sea urchins over there.**
    F. **I've found no sand dollars this week.**
    G. **There is scarcely anybody on the beach.**
    H. **I can't see through my goggles neither.**
    I. **I ain't got no lunch money.**

Use the sentences below to answer 67–70.
    J. **Many fish eat algae for food.**
    K. **Swimming is great exercise.**
    L. **To catch a lobster, you need a good trap.**
    M. **Testing to see if the water was cold, John stuck his toes in slowly.**

_____ 67. Which sentence has a prepositional phrase? Name the preposition. _____

_____ 68. Which sentence has a participle? Name the participle. _____

_____ 69. Which sentence has a gerund? Name the gerund. _____

_____ 70. Which sentences have infinitives? Name the infinitives. _____

For each sentence, tell whether the clause is **(I) independent,** or **(S) subordinate** (dependent).

_____ 71. the tide is out

_____ 72. when we buried Todd in the sand

_____ 73. since she left the boardwalk

_____ 74. you should get out of the water

Tell whether each clause in bold print is a noun, adjective, or adverb clause.

_____ 75. Anyone could join the scuba class **which was scheduled for Tuesday.**

_____ 76. Anna is the teenager **who is the owner of the umbrella.**

_____ 77. **Before I swim here,** I want to make sure there are no sharks.

_____ 78. The shop **that rents jet skis** is open all day.

_____ 79. **Whenever I dive near a sunken ship,** I feel a sense of mystery.

_____ 80. **Whoever comes to the picnic** will be well fed.

_____ 81. She screamed **as if she were being swallowed by a whale.**

Name _____

For 82–89, tell whether the word in bold print is a **direct object (D)** or an **indirect object (I)**.

_____ 82. The barracuda ate the **diver.**

_____ 83. The lifeguard signaled **Joe** a warning.

_____ 84. I sent my **boyfriend** a letter in a bottle.

_____ 85. Jonathan ate clam **chowder.**

_____ 86. Brie handed **me** a hermit crab.

_____ 87. The whale gave us a great **show.**

_____ 88. That last wave gave Brad a **ride** all the way to the beach.

_____ 89. An old pirate showed **us** some buried treasure.

For 90–100, correct each sentence to give it the correct capitalization and punctuation.

90. when is high tide james asked the lifeguard at main street beach

_____

91. high tide he answered is around 3 15 p m today

_____

92. moby dick is my favorite novel of all announced nick

_____

93. roberto the oceanographer is from san juan puerto rico

_____

94. usually sea anemones starfish and fiddler crabs all hang around tide pools

_____

95. governor wilson read the sunday beach times on malibu beach

_____

96. there were seven beach chairs left we had eight people

_____

97. a canadian diver said he would dive off the golden gate bridge on new years day

_____

98. she told me of ginas accomplishments 6 world championships 8 u s championships and 7 olympic gold medals

_____

99. the winds are rising and the seas waves are angry it must mean a storm is coming

_____

100. wait i left my copy of the old man and the sea on the beach

_____

SCORE: Total Points _____ out of a possible 100 points

Name _____